Copyright © 2011 by M. Susan Deaton

All Rights Reserved. No part of this book my be reproduced or transmitted   in any form or by any means without permission in writing from the author.

I dedicate this book to my husband Keith

Introduction

The following book contains reflections, drawings, and poetry about my life's journey, which touches many areas of my life. These journeys embrace my faith and is my grounding for understanding the interconnections of the world around me.

I started my journey with my family and their ideologies and tradition. I grew up with a mother who loved to read and paint and a dad who dedicated his life to my security. My first perception of the world was through their eyes and their judgments. I think one of the perceptions instilled in me from my mother was an attitude of independence. Like her, I needed to be strong in my opinions and judge the world on my terms, through my beliefs, and most of all through my faith. If I had to define the core of myself, I would define it through the eyes of faith. Although, my journey has taken me away from the formal religion embedded in my mother and father's faith, I still maintain my faith nonetheless. It is through the sureness of the seasons and the strength of the trees and mountains that I find God. I believe if we open ourselves to the beauty of the world around us, we can find the faith that naturally exist in our being. Much of my art is a reflection of my faith. I feel as though my drawings are prayers, a celebration of the beauty that exists and is woven through my life. I have a deep-seated love for nature, which reflects my faith in God. Finding beauty and for that matter ugliness has been a life-long pursuit of understanding. It would seem that the ability to comprehend beauty is the same as trying to comprehend God, in that there are meanings beyond our grasp.

I believe the deeper people explores and observe the world around them the more connections they make to the complexity that makes up the world. I find this to be true for myself. These deep connections are a direct result of my love and ability to draw what I see. I believe that drawing as a means of knowing, seeing, and understanding is grossly under valued in our scientifically minded society.

In the first section of this book, I've included examples of the types of drawings I do. Although I explain what the drawing means to me, I invite you to come to your own conclusions. The second half of this books includes both drawings and poetry. I don't think of the art that accompanies the poems as illustrations of the poems unless I noted otherwise. I simply placed the art and the poem together because they were similar in subject. There are a few drawings that are presented with a title only.

I hope my expressions will assist you as you explore yours.

M. Susan Deaton

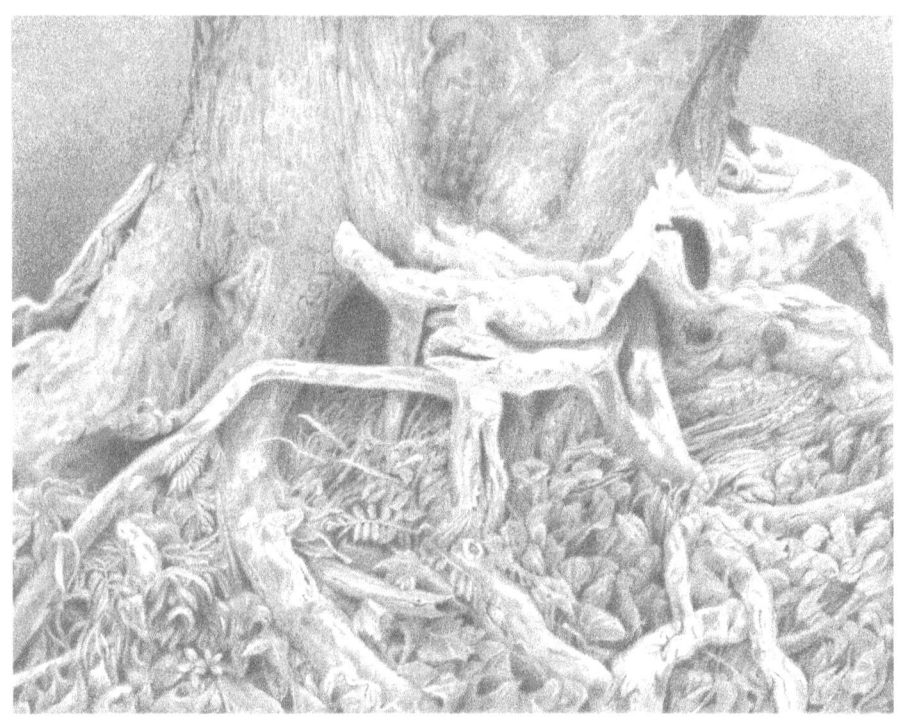

The Memory of the Cumberland

"The Memory of the Cumberland" reflects my love of nature. I have always enjoyed finding my way through the woods and exploring the banks of the river. I think the search for the picture I draw is as enjoyable and as exciting as doing the drawing itself.

Through my explorations, I have discovered the stories Mother Nature tells. "The Memory of the Cumberland" tells a story as much about the Cumberland river as the tree. The tree's roots are exposed because the river swells each spring washing away a layer of soil. The tree becomes a unique living sculpture as a response to the temperamental river. The two become intertwined in their beauty, telling a dramatic story about life and survival.

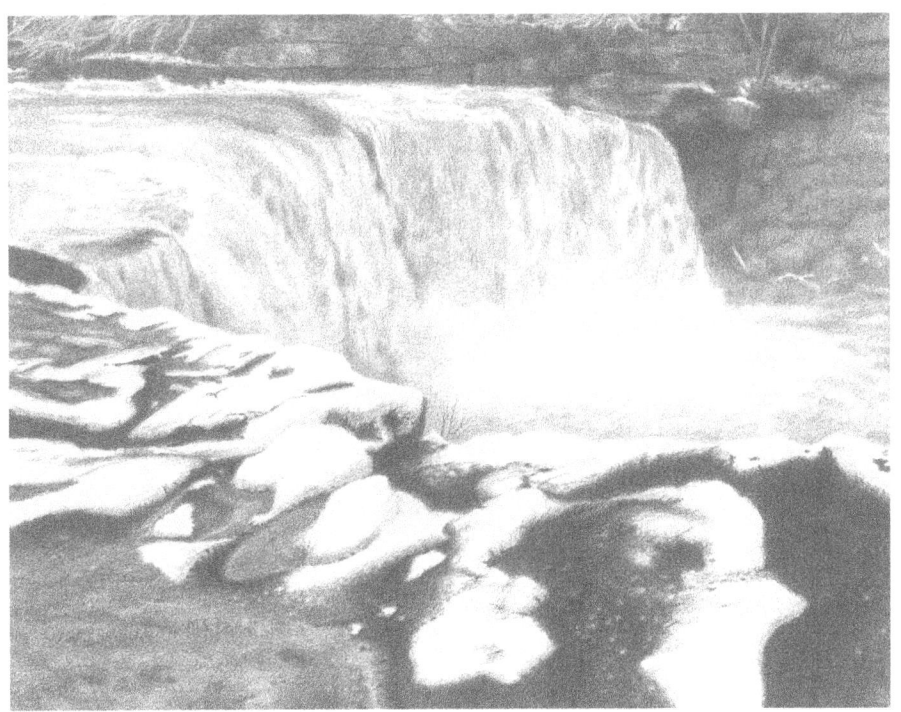

Winter Falls

Cumberland Falls is a park near my home in southeastern Kentucky. I go there often and walk along the river. Over the years it has become a special place for me to go to find inspirations as an artist. Before drawing this picture of the falls in the snow, I had no ambition to do a drawing of the falls. It's interesting how the seasons can influence our perception and make something that seemed so stereotypical become unique. The world is constantly changing, what is common on one day becomes unique on another.

Another place that has inspired much of my art and poetry is the Red River Gorge. The drawing "The Faces of Red River" (page 20) and the poem define one of my favorite places. I have spent more that half my life exploring the gorge and never tire of its changing beauty.

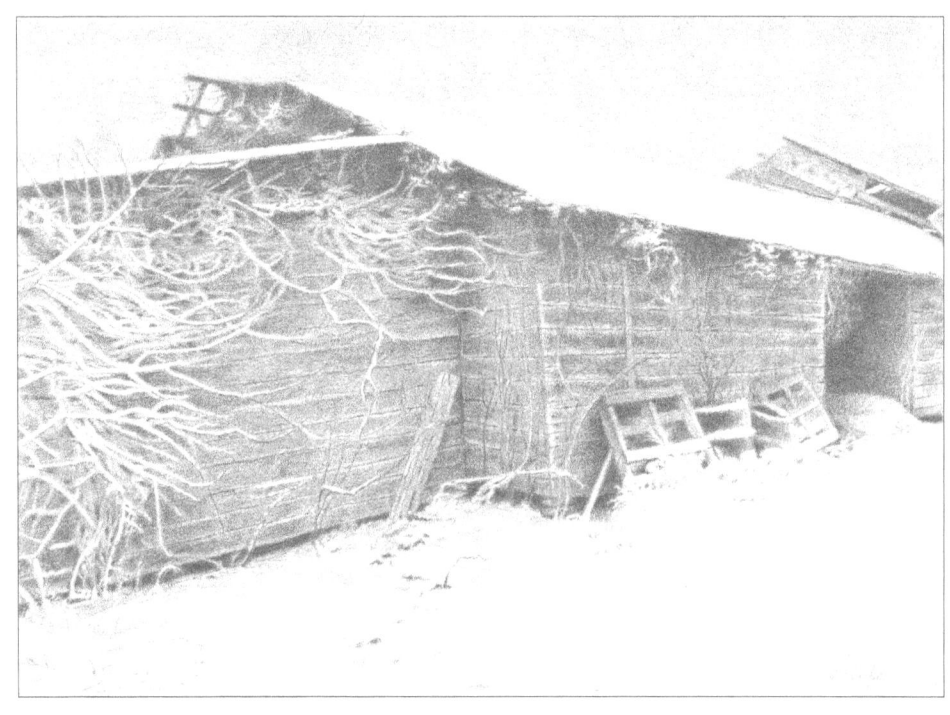

A Gift for Mary Francis

I've taken photographs of this barn in autumn and winter. I suppose I should comment on the fact that I do many of my drawings from photographs I've taken. As I've mentioned, finding the right "picture" is as enjoyable to me as is drawing. There is nothing more exciting than finding that perfect photograph that will translate to a drawing or painting. What could be better than a weathered barn with its lights and dark buried in the delicateness of new snow.

The title of this drawing is in memory of my Aunt Mary Francis. She painted all her life and had a strong influence on me. She loved to paint birds, buffalos, and barns in the snow. It's interesting how the things we find beautiful are sweet memories or connections we have to the people we love. I'm quite sure that this picture is beautiful for me because my Aunt Mary Francis's artistic commitment to rustic old barns. The family connections we have run deep into our perceptions of the world and define the way we see it and choose to express it. I am indebted to my Aunt Mary Francis and my mother for establishing art as a means of expression for my ideas and view of the world.

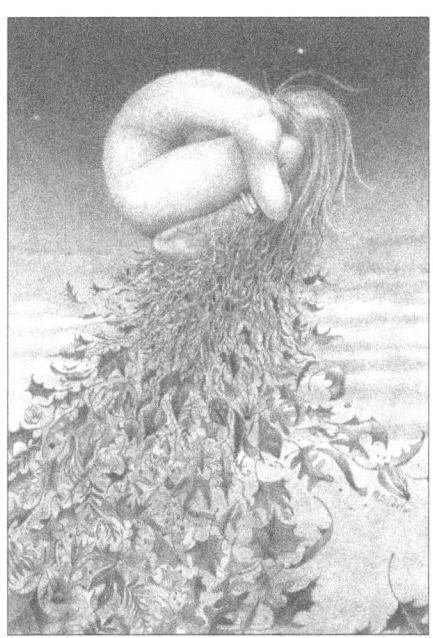

The Middle of Time

In addition to creating an illusion of space on a page, I enjoy developing an image that uniquely expresses a bigger idea that is not readily interpreted. Like Bosch, Dali, and Escher, a few of my favorite artists, I like to inject a deeper meaning to my art. "The Middle of Time" represent the moments we live in between our past and our future. When I look back over my journal entries, the emotional patterns that emerge are embedded in my need to relive the past or in my planning for the future—looking at all the possibilities of what could be. I find myself wasting my time doing one or the other. So the "Middle of Time" has almost become the symbol for myself... my goal for living. I want to find myself in the present and enjoy what each moment has to offer. Maybe I could go so far as to say that is what an artist is—someone who lives and celebrates the present.

I believe that God lives in the present, which is why I love to walk along the river and explore the woods—this is my time to listen to God. I think the creation of my art is my response to God. In other words my drawings, paintings, and poetry are my prayers of joy, of sadness, of outrage, and most of all thankfulness. I believe God expresses love through the beauty of the mountains, trees, and sky. The entire epic of creation lives out each day if we only take the time to listen with our ears, eyes, and hearts.

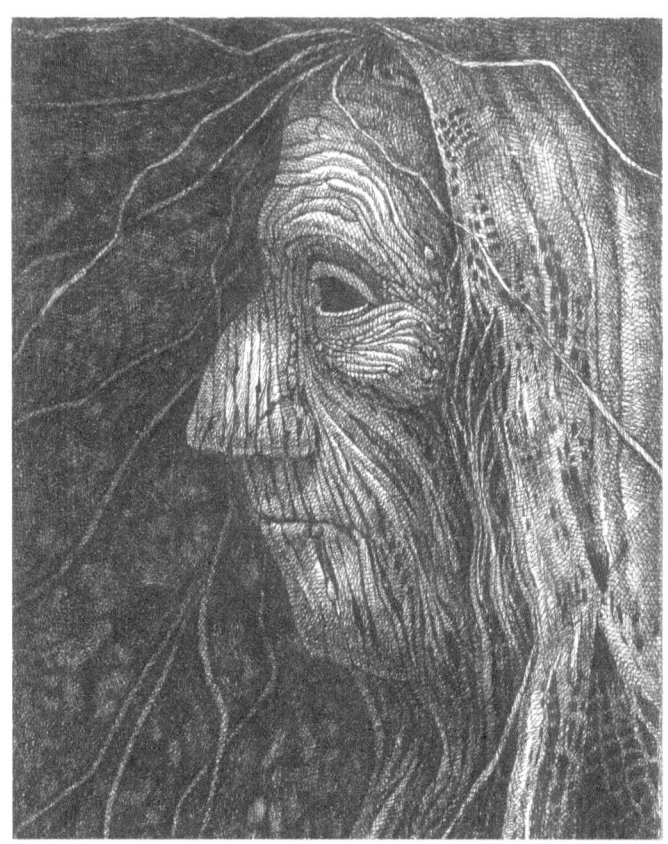

Petrified Soul

I suppose the artist Rene' Magritte inspired this image. At the time I did this drawing, I was working with lines and shades, creating an illusion of space as representational and non- representational compositions. I have an entire series of these pen and ink drawing. It's interesting to review the kind of art I've done over the years and compare them to where I am now. I have definitely learned and taken those morsels of techniques and images and continue to use them. I guess nothing we do is really worthless—it all teaches us something about something.

Petrified Soul represents the kind of images I like to do with pen and ink. I find that I use pen and ink for emotionally dramatic pictures. I think the most imaginative pictures I draw are the ones that represent the deeper ideas I have about fairness, justice or the deep emotions I feel about life.

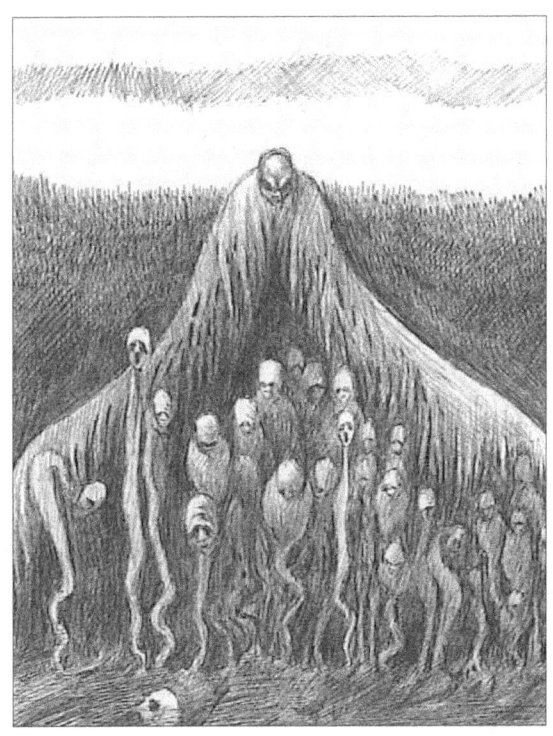

Mythologies of Power

I drew the "Mythologies of Power" after a visit to the Holocaust Museum in Washington D.C. I'm not really sure how this image evolved—other than my desire to create a pure symbol or expression of an idea about injustice. I have several drawing of these "stem people" that I've used to help describe feelings of outrage or unfairness. I suppose this image and the others I've done are a part of my repertoire of expression. It's interesting how drawing the beautiful form of an apple is so simple and direct. When I am representing the ugliness of humanity, however, it is by its very nature a symbolic abstraction. It is the inner construction of our minds that create our idea of goodness or evil.

The "Mythologies of Power" is a drawing that represents the ideologies that influence the way we think about the world and each other. We all define ourselves by what we choose to believe and it is through these beliefs that we take action. Sometimes these beliefs and actions are unjust, yet, we are blind to the injustice. It is as if we live under an umbrella of darkness, only seeing what is under the umbrella and no further.

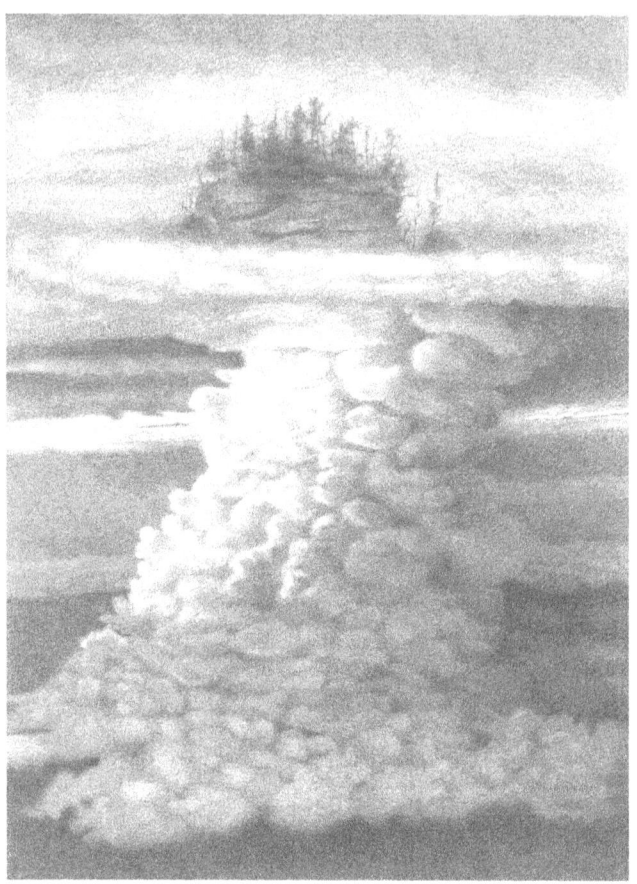

Do Stripped Mined Mountains go to Heaven?

"Do Strip Mined Mountains Go to Heaven?" coincides with my love of nature in that the picture asks a question about the results of our actions as a society. As a society we are so immersed in our own salvation, yet we seem to have little regard for the natural environment that sustains us. Maybe I'm hoping for the same guilt we fashion for ourselves to apply to our apathy toward the earth.

Mountain Top Removal is a hideous practice of coal mining that destroys the incredible diversity and beauty of the mountains. Some call it Mountain Range Removal. As human beings we are creative and have developed some of the most wonderful inventions in human history. I have complete confidence that as a society we can develop alternative fuel sources and stop this hideous practice.

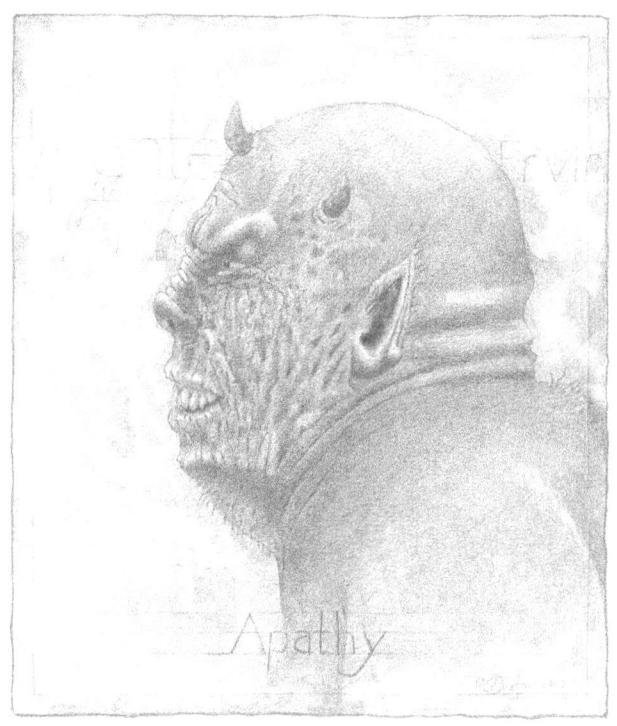

Apathy

The drawing of "Apathy" is a follow-up to "Do Stripped Mined Mountains go to Heaven". The idea for the drawing emerged more than 20 years ago when I attended a Dante Institute sponsored by the National Endowment for the Humanities. We studied the "Divine Comedy" and the culture and politics of the Middle Ages. As a project, I illustrated several cantos, from "The Inferno". Canto XXI intrigued me most. It describes black demons with pitch forks. "They were like cooks who make their scullery boys poke down into the caldron with their forks to keep the meat from floating to the top." I drew a picture of demons with their pitch forks and the bobbing "meat". I researched to find out how the people of the middle ages depicted demons and started my drawing from there. I used my knowledge of the skeletal structure of the human head to transform human features into the grotesque. I gave these original drawings away years ago. However, I resurrected this image to represent the apathy in our society that permits so much destruction to our environment..

Art and Poetry

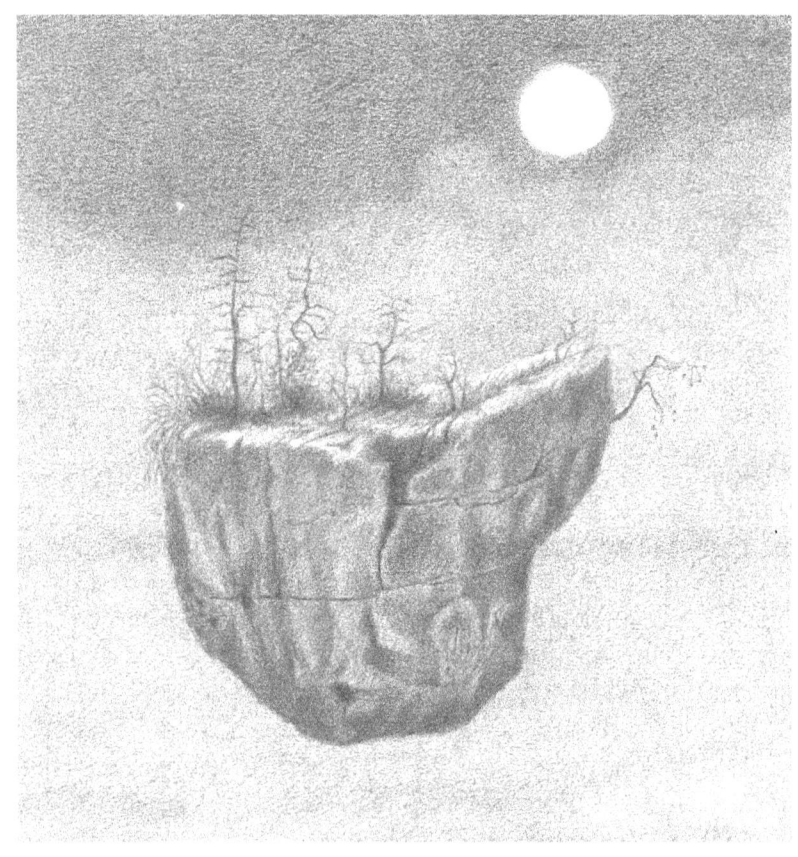

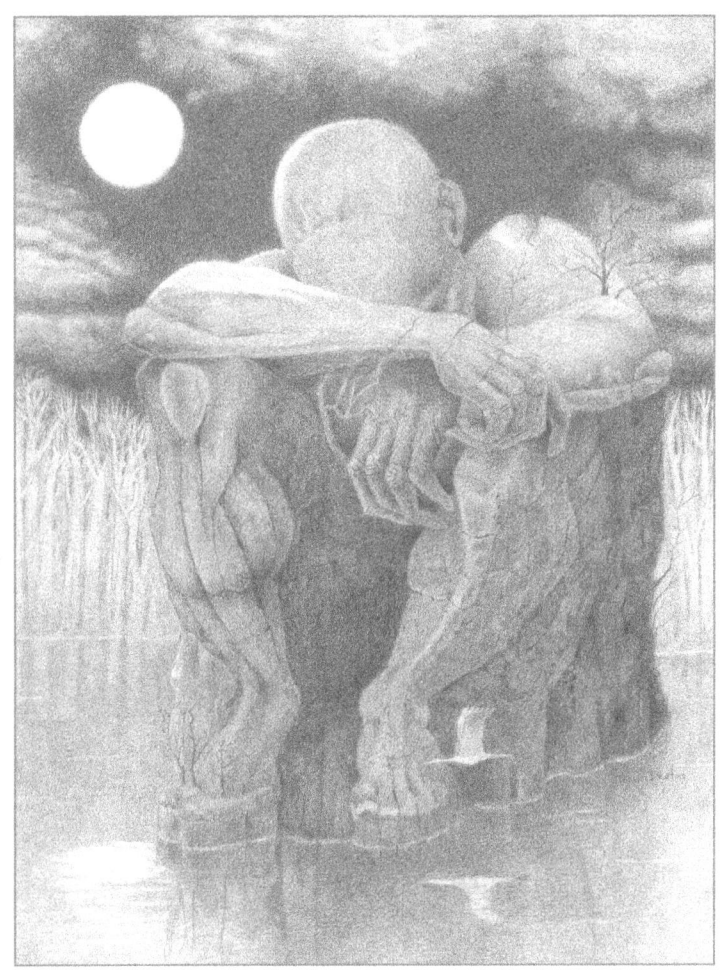

Deep Time

The high cliffs of southeastern Kentucky look down on the meager life

surrounding them. It is as though they sleep

as we go about our busy lives.

They never seem to notice the hawks that soar overhead

or the generations of trees that live

and die on their shoulders. Nor do they notice the wind and water

that chisels away their features, leaving them unique monuments of time.

(written to describe the picture)

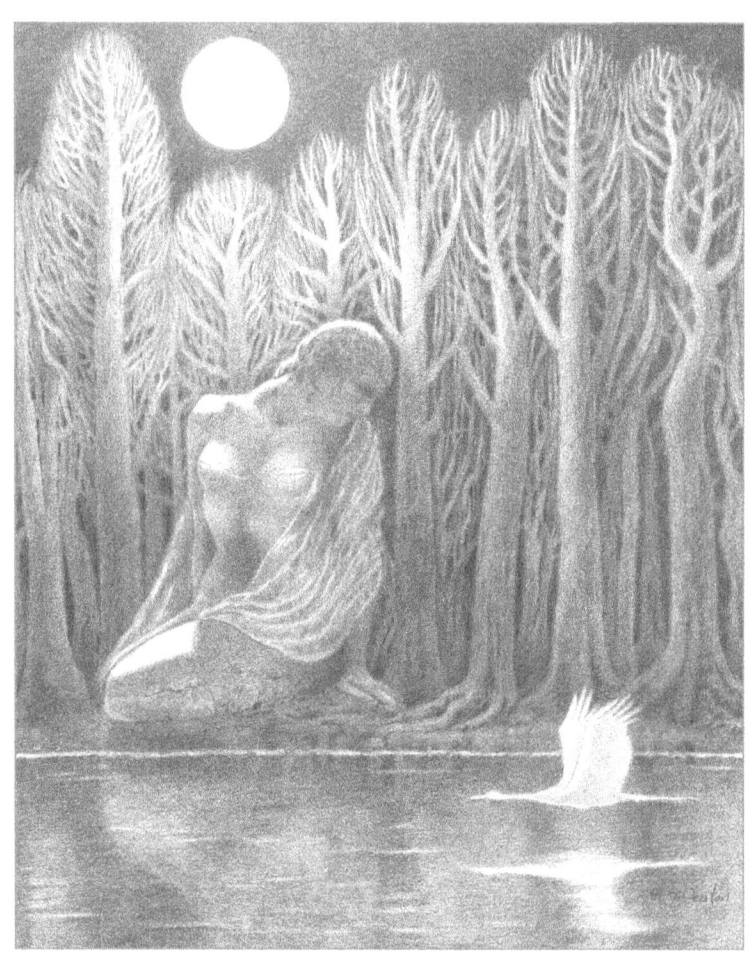

The Meadow

A leftover whisper from the moon
still sleeps on the meadow
as the soft transition
between night and light opens
the embrace of the sycamore.
A crow flies with the hint of lavender,
calling for the whispers to wake and see.

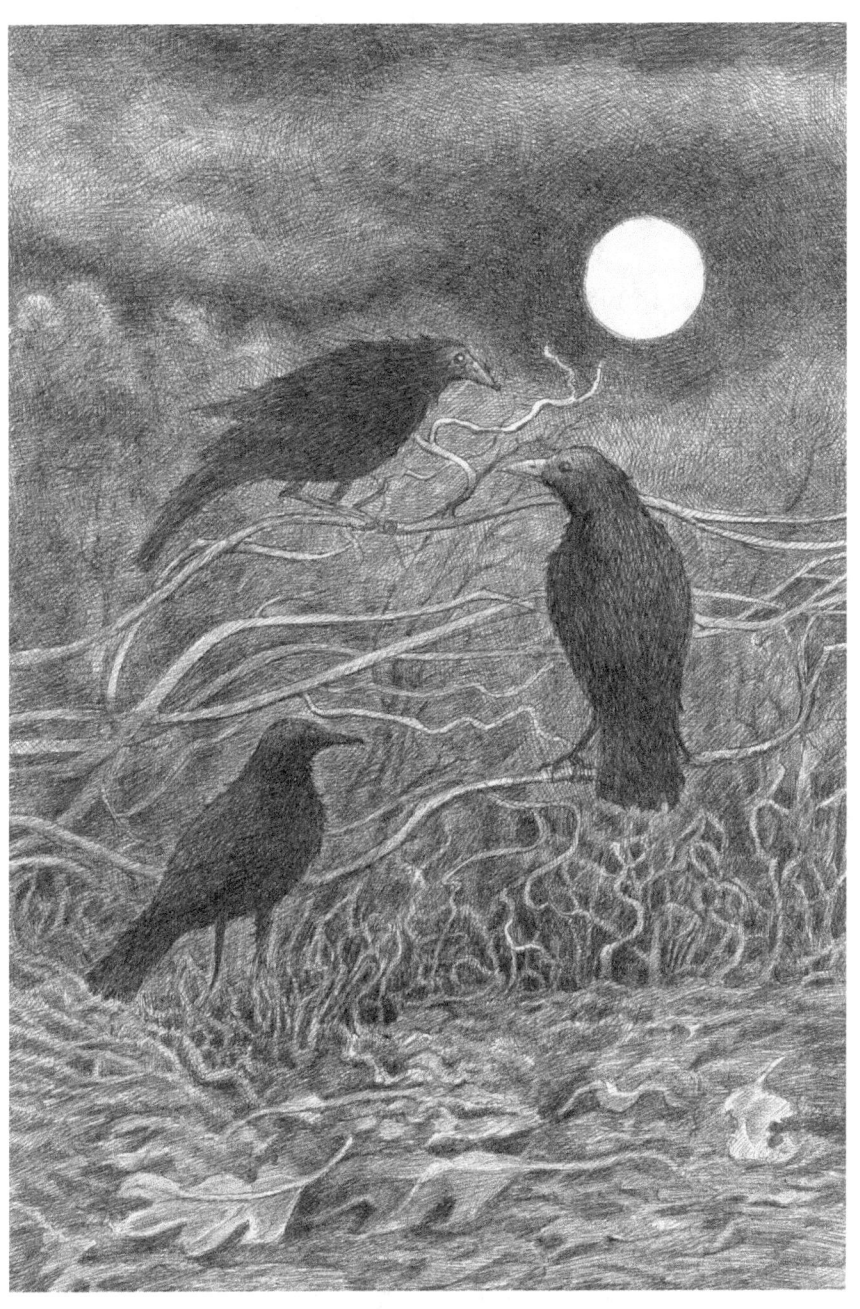

Keeping the Wind in its Rage

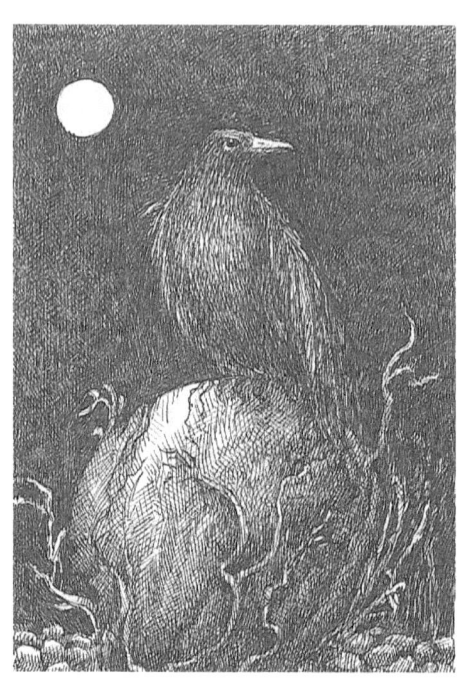

Awake

A single call of a scavenger
awakens my darkness.
Forcing me, again
to feel the rough path
and hear the morning sky
as it rushes through the fingers of the earth.
The crow seems to scorn me
for losing my purpose.
Forgetting, why
I needed a breath of honesty
and a touch of certainty,
why the delicate tissues of my being
were screaming for freedom.

The Journey

The pine, orphaned

with its broken arms

and withered seeds,

becomes the magnificent.

A dark skeleton, against

the dying heaven,

a death that burns

with the passion

of simmering coals.

My breath becomes a breath, shared

with the eternity of colors

and the prayers that wish a moment

could last forever.

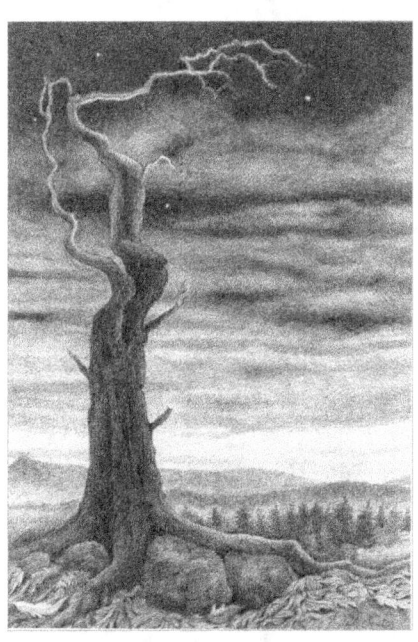

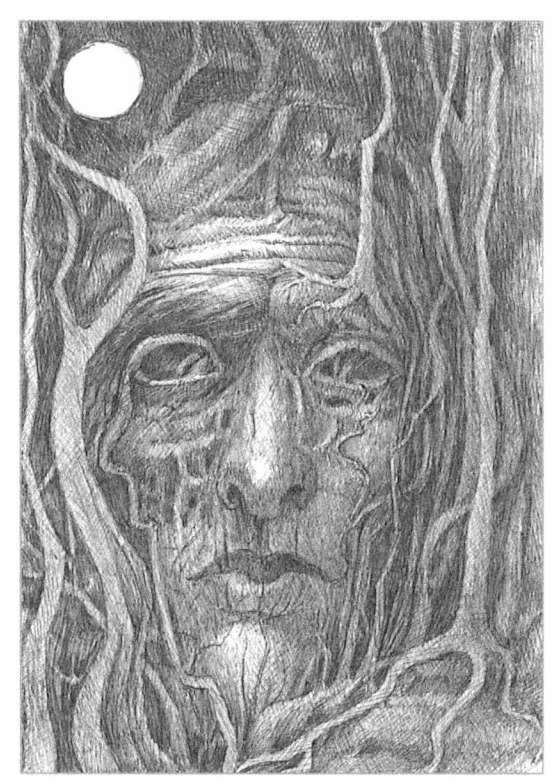

The Faces of Red River

Faces scatter

and open their expression

to the velvety touch of moss

and the board shiny leaves of the magnolia.

They cradle the delicate fern

in their solid grasp;

and hold their place

as the roots of the maple trees

dig to find the riches they cannot offer.

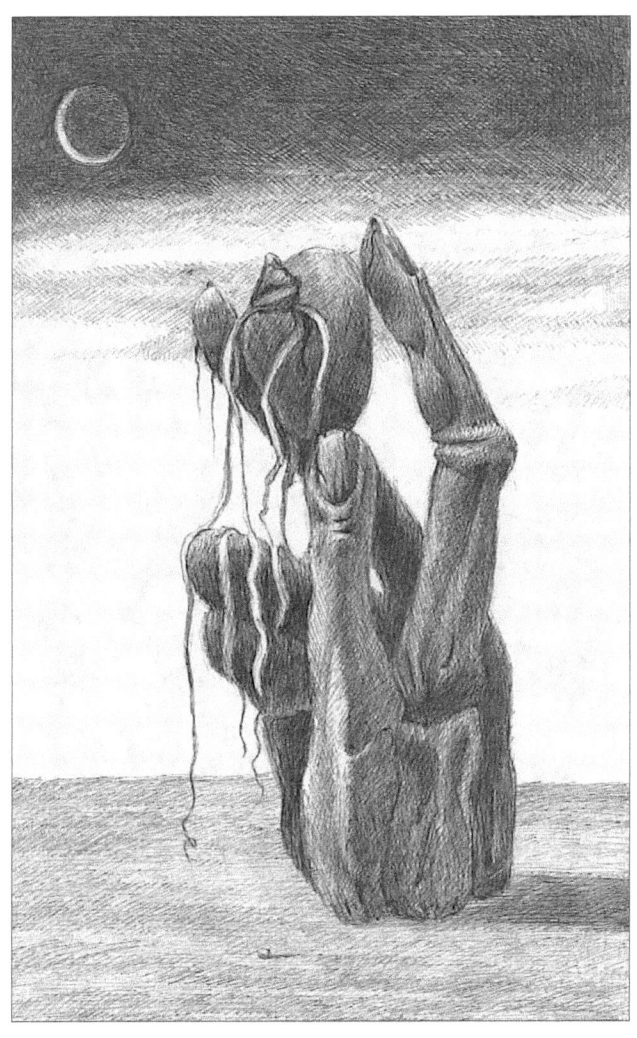

To Touch a Moment

Before the sparrows wake,
before the glow from windows
disturb the darkness,
I walk through the middle of time.
I breathe in the moment
and exhale the warmth of my being
into the blank new sky.

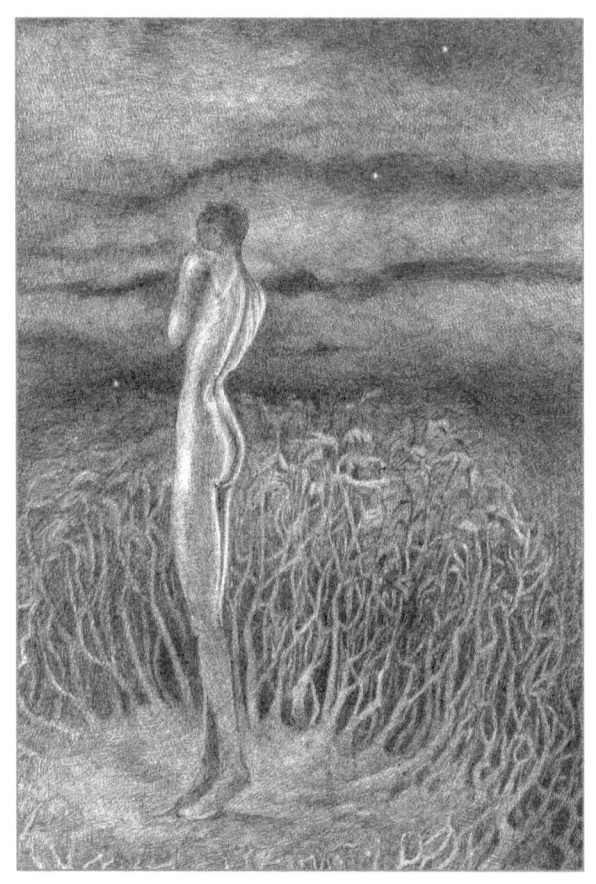

A Mother's Secret

I touched the tarnished brass, gently
so not to disturb her knowing,
for trust's precious bond
holds its bounty in the silence.
Only a glimpse will confirm asleep
the living being that is my heart.

I close the door as gently, relieved,
for the world has returned her to me.

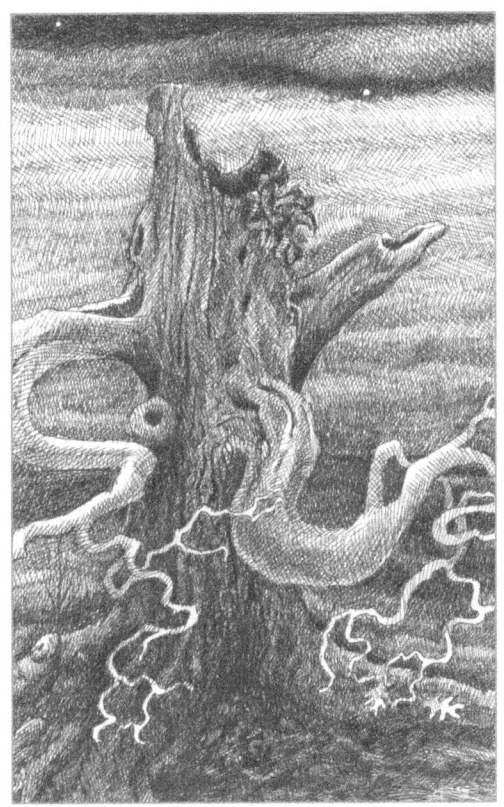

Beauty

The meanings
are my legacy from the earth,
woven through my eyes
and bound to my beating heart.
Dormant,
until the cool silence of winter
beckons the pastel sky to speak.
My eyes listen and understand,
leaving my mind aware of a language
it will never grasp.

A December Journey

The bare trees cradle
the long night moon
as the clouds weave a tapestry
of fading colors.
   *

The sky holds no memory
as a blue veil shroud covers the silence
that awakens in the cool winter ashes.
   *

The long night moon
brings sureness to the darkness
leading the stars
to impose their mystery.

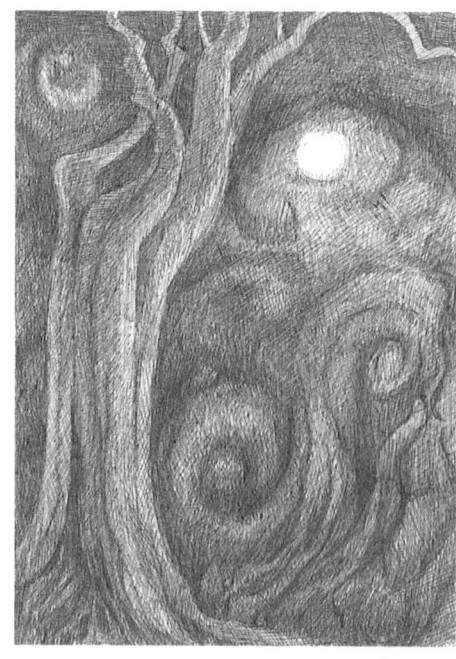

Morning Roads

The road finds the edge of the world
as the sun's thirst consumes the mist
born in the sweet air shadow of the earth.

The blazing spectacle forces my sight inward,
finding the prayer said without a word,
within the eternity of a moment.

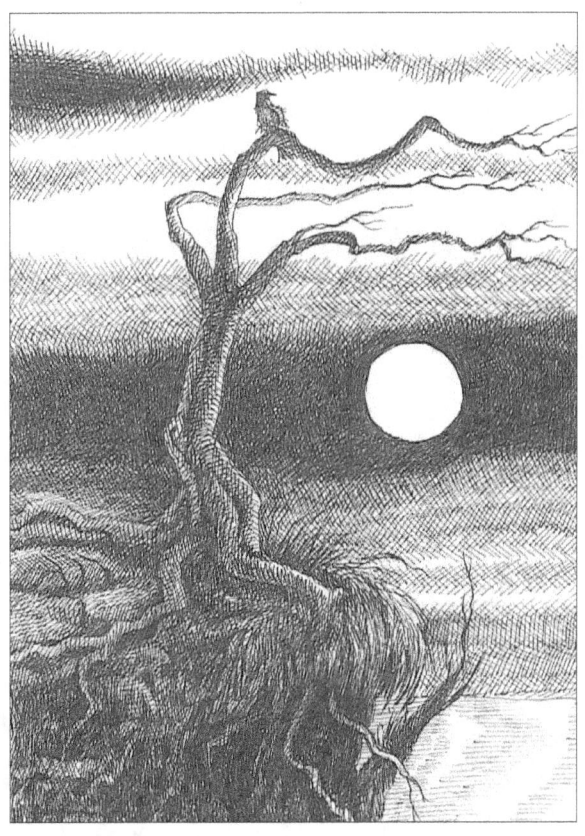

Life

The sapling begins
in the deep light of life
where the sun and the breeze
tease the shadows.
The seedling is bound
by the dead debris of seasons,
fragile
even to the speechless sky.
Confidently, it stretches
into the universe of colorful prayers
and burrows deep
into the darkness of faith.

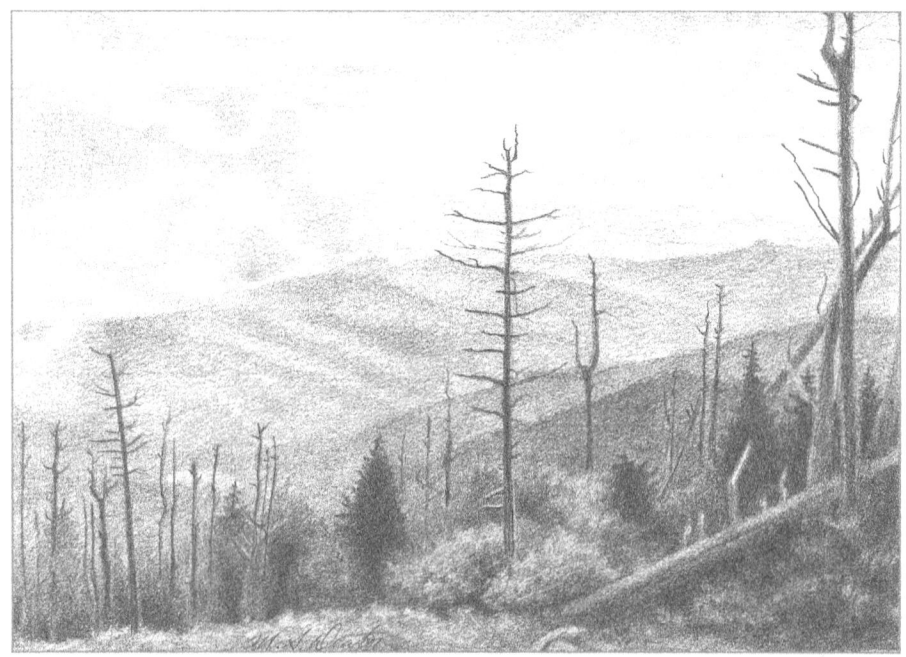

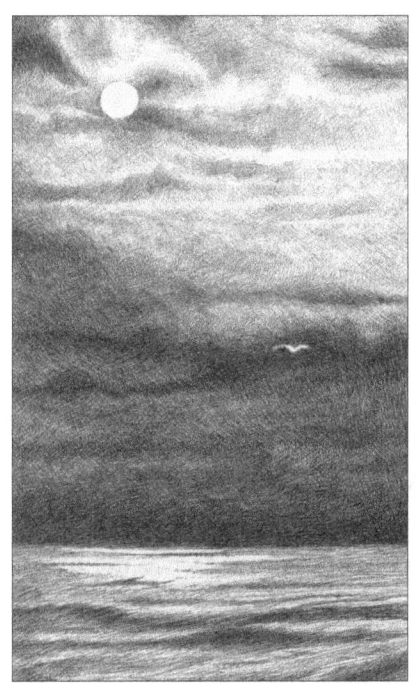

An Eternity with No Memory

The salty foam

 delicately touches

the ancient edge of silence.

Its love's roar rolls,

capping its crescent victory with white lace

pouring out its caress—

with no hesitation

it falls back into its deathless rhythm—

with the silence,

holding no memory

of my footsteps.

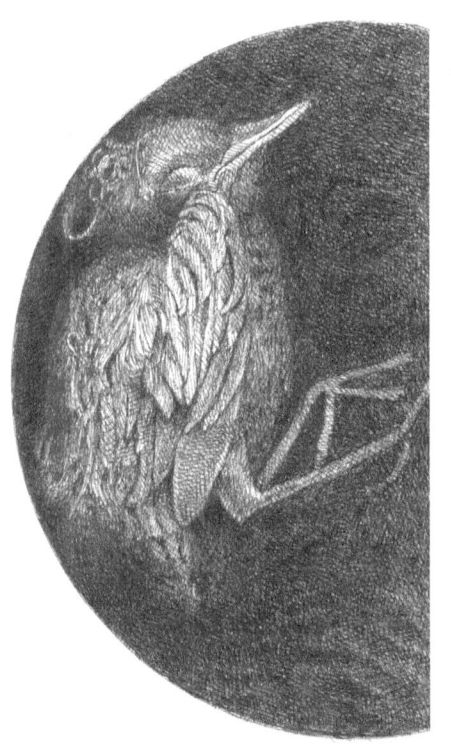

A Life of Chances

The silhouette of a sparrow, settles
in the center of a streetlight's gaze,
caught outside of day,
she waits
for the stars to leave.
What instinct betrayed her?
Leaving her stranded
on this pavement of chances.

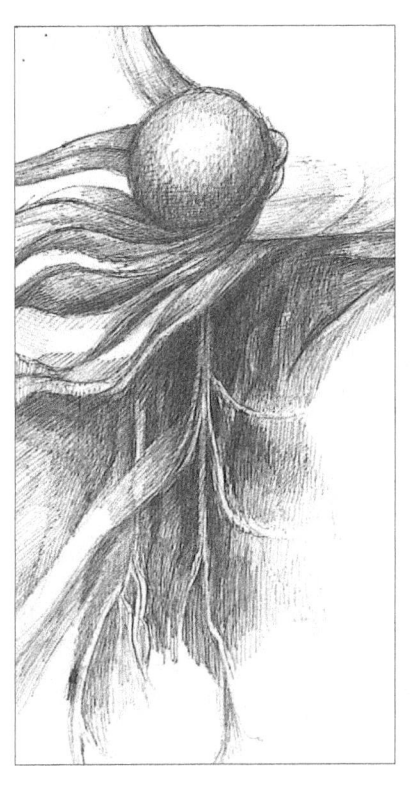

Winter Flowers

Love always remembers to love.
It finds every face and every
heart familiar. Love is not afraid
of the uncertainty of a name,
it forever finds its meaning
and blooms.

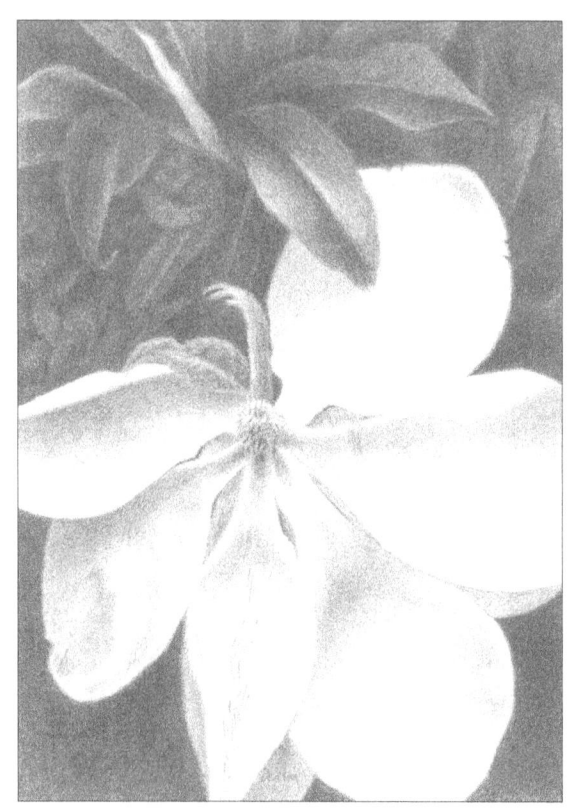

Chris
(1963-1987)

Stillness consuming its meaning
in my brother's face.
The sacred words cannot be heard
for the stillness is so loud!

It ignores the pleas from my tears
and pushes me away.
Leaving memory's remnants
to clothe my naked heart.

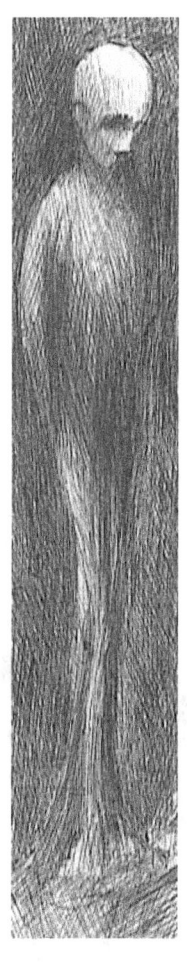

June

A single sparrow's song
is all the heavy breath of July affords
for this burying day.
Like the distant thunder,
the preacher's prayer
is deep and certain.

My tears find their place
as the hazy shadow of the mountain
embraces its love.

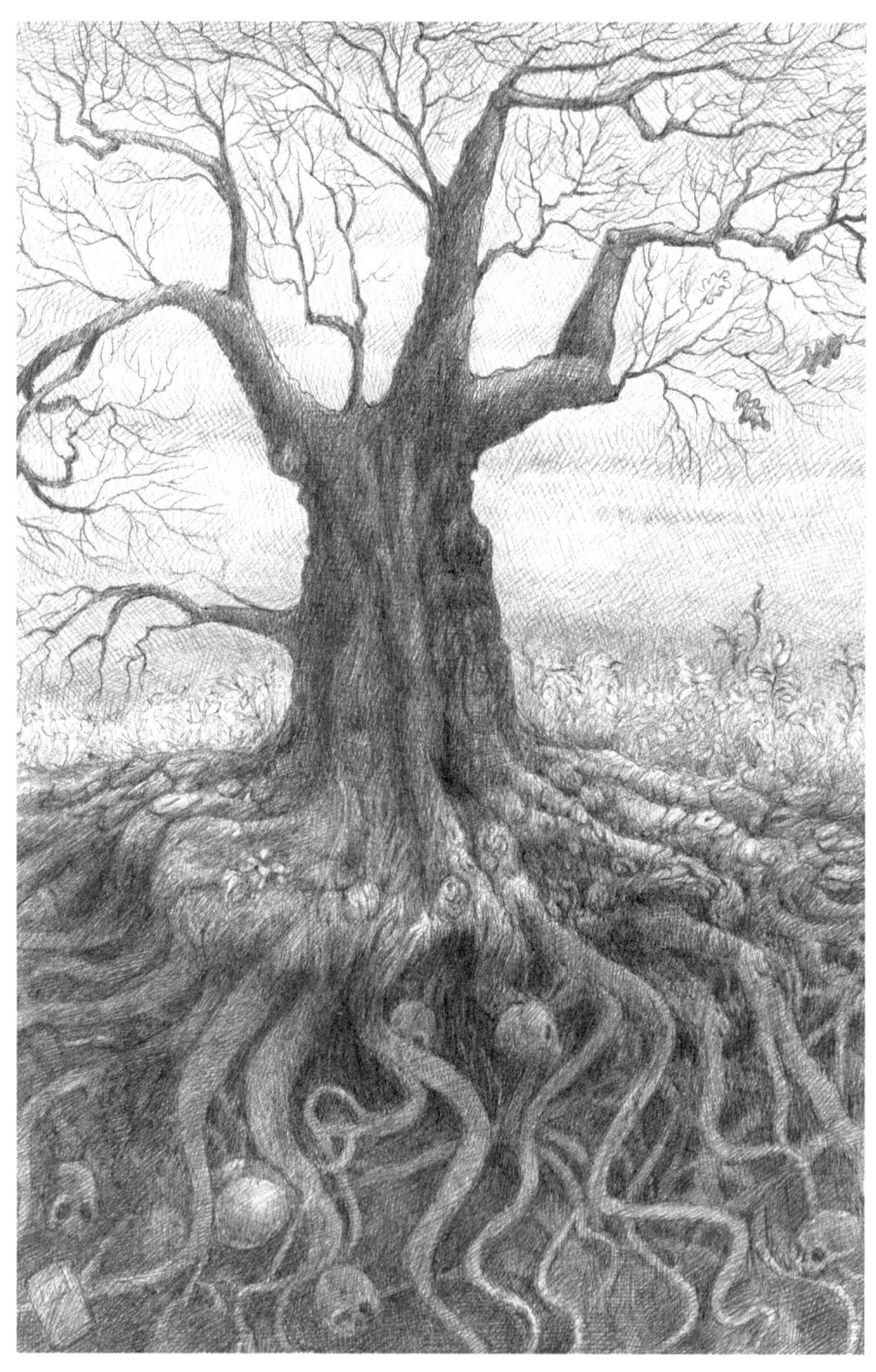

History's Heap

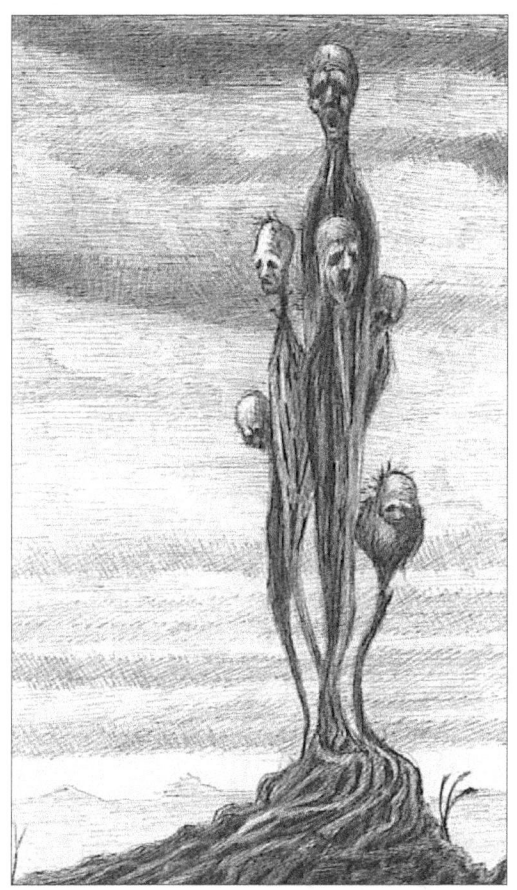

The Ghosts of St. Johns, Indiana

Their footsteps have been cleansed from the dirt,
    their whispers carried away by the wind.
        Their memories ask
           "what darkness moved the trees
        and the contour of the sky?"

      The darkness has no reply.

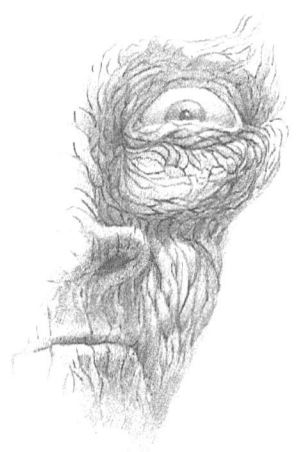

Wasteland
(Mountain Top Removal)

They split open the month of June
and gut her eternity,
leaving the autumn rain
to pour down the naked wound.
The winter winds lash and weep
for their familiar caress—only to find the shadows
of rocks and mud, the blood of heaven.
With April's fragile memory
they plant grass on the corpse
hoping to fool the horizon, hoping
to hide their sin.

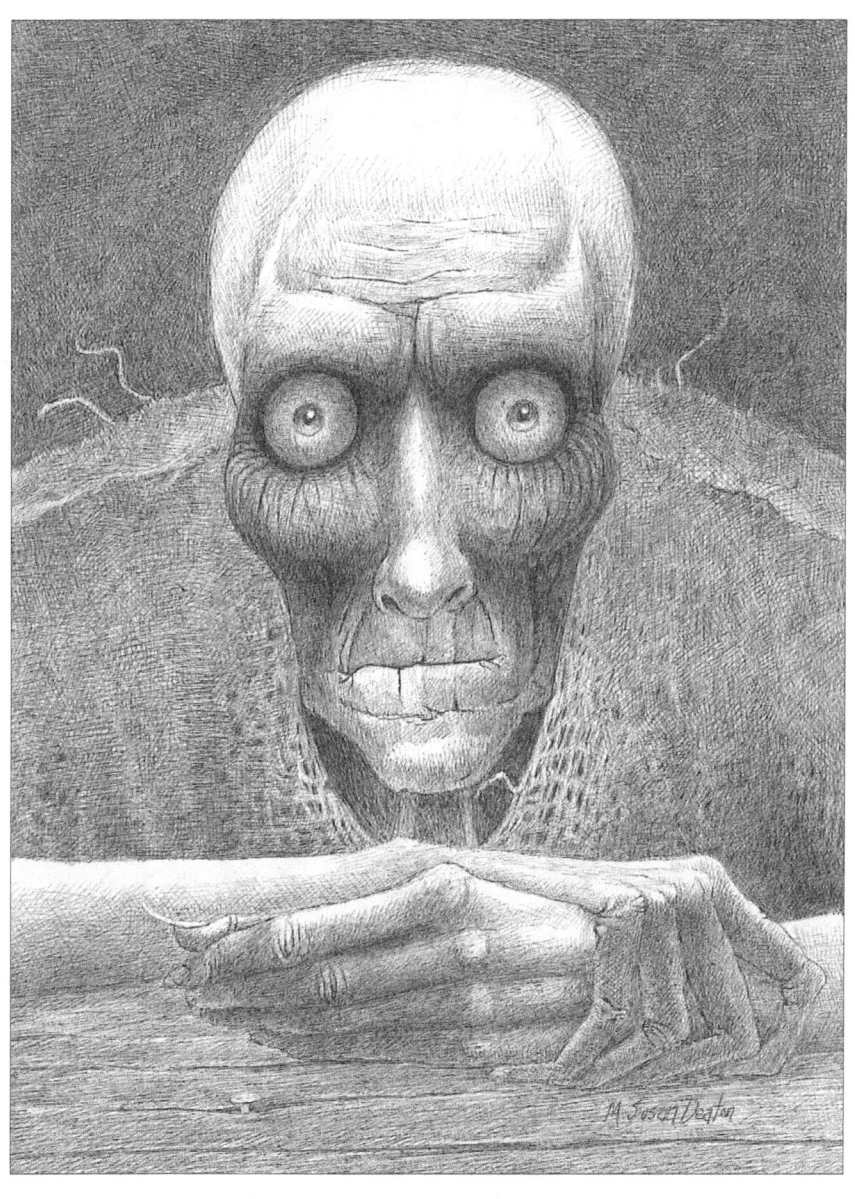

The Vigilant Keeper of the Status Quo
His answers
are the only answers,
his love is the only love,
and his hate is absolute.

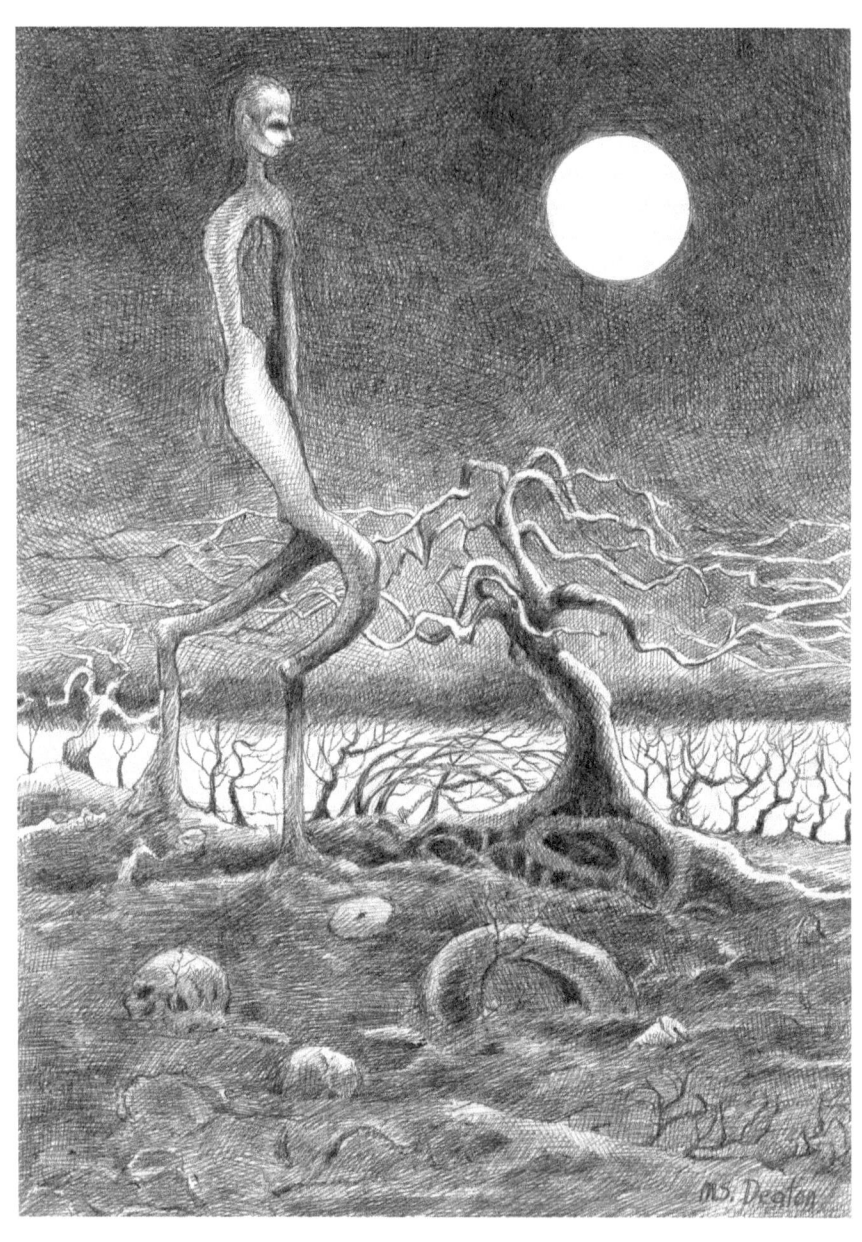

Habits of Mind

www.ingramcontent.com/pod-product-compliance
Lightning Source LLC
Chambersburg PA
CBHW030103230526
45471CB00003B/1237